EARTH CYCLES

ROCKS

Sally Morgan

W

FRANKLIN WATTS

LONDON•SYDNEY

First published in 2009 by Franklin Watts
338 Euston Road
London NW1 3BH

Franklin Watts Australia
Level 17/207 Kent Street
Sydney, NSW 2000

Editor: Jean Coppendale
Design: Paul Manning

Produced for Franklin Watts by
White-Thomson Publishing Ltd

www.wtpub.co.uk
+44 (0) 845 362 8240

A CIP catalogue record for this book is available from the British Library.

ISBN 978 0 7496 8839 4

Dewey classification 552

Picture credits

t = top b = bottom l = left = r = right
Cover main, 1, 8m, Shutterstock/Julien Grondin; cover m, 23l, ECO/Fritz Polking; cover b, 9t, Shutterstock/Kavram; cover t, 9r, Shutterstock/John A. Andersen; 3l, 23r, ECO/Fritz Polking; 3r, 8l, Shutterstock/Sam D. Cruz; 4, Shutterstock/Marek Gahura-Uniolife; 5l, ECO/Anthony Cooper; 5b, Shutterstock/Peter Weber; 5m, Shutterstock/N. Frey Photography; 5r, Shutterstock/Paula Cobleigh; 6, Shutterstock/Andrea Danti; 7l, ECO/Chinch Gryniewicz; 7t, Shutterstock/Morozova Tatyana (Manamana); 7r, Stefan Chabluk; 8t, Shutterstock/Keysurfing; 8b, Shutterstock/Annmarie Young; 9b, Shutterstock/Kavram; 10b, Shutterstock/Julien Grondin; 10t, Stefan Chabluk; 11l, ECO/Sally Morgan; 11t, Shutterstock/Adrian 507; 11b, Mila Zinkova; 12, Shutterstock/David Thyberg; 13l, Shutterstock/Liudmila Cherniak; 13r, Shutterstock/Steve Maehl; 14t, ECO/Robert Pickett; 14b, Shutterstock/Derek F. Smith; 15, Shutterstock/Nickolay Stanev; 16, 31, Shutterstock/Bluecrayola; 17t, ECO/Richard Glover; 17m, ECO/Wayne Lawler; 17b, ECO/Phillip Colla; 17r, ECO/Kjell Sandved; 18, Shutterstock/Romeo Sparrow; 18, Stefan Chabluk; 19l, Stefan Chabluk; 19r, Shutterstock/RobertPaul van Beets; 20, Shutterstock/David Woods; 20t, Shutterstock/David Woods; 21l, Shutterstock/Roberto Marinello; 21t, Shutterstock/Kevin Britland; 21b, Shutterstock/4745052183; 22, ECO/Fritz Polking; 24, Shutterstock/Maugli; 25l, John Farmar; 25r, Shutterstock/Terry Kettlewell; 26, Shutterstock/Noam Armonn; 26t, Shutterstock/Brandon Blinkenberg; 27l, ECO/Chinch Gryniewicz; 27r, ECO/Peter Hulme; 28, Shutterstock/Roca; 29l, ECO/Jim Winkley; 29m, ECO/Latha Raman; 29r, Shutterstock/Evan Meyer.

Note to parents and teachers

Every effort has been made by the Publishers to ensure that the websites listed on page 32 are suitable for children, that they are of the highest educational value and that they contain no inappropriate or offensive material. However, because of the nature of the Internet, it is impossible to guarantee that the contents of these sites will not been altered. We strongly advise that Internet access is supervised by a responsible adult.

Printed in China

Franklin Watts is a division of Hachette Children's Books,
an Hachette UK company
www.hachette.co.uk

Contents

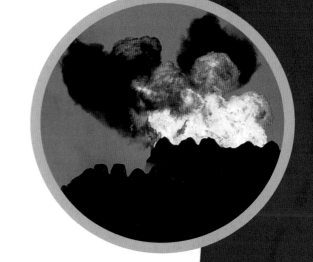

Words appearing in **bold** can
be found in the Glossary
on pages 30-31.

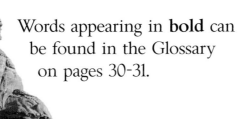

What are rocks?

The ground beneath our feet is the surface of the Earth's outer layer or **crust**. This layer is made up entirely of rocks. Most rocks are hard, and they come in a range of colours from white through to green and black.

Minerals

Rocks are made of **minerals** that occur naturally in the ground. Some rocks are made up of a single mineral, such as **limestone**, which contains **calcium carbonate**. Others are made up of several minerals, for example **granite** contains **quartz**, **feldspar** and **biotite**.

Rock groups

Rocks are placed in three groups, according to how they were formed. These groups are **igneous**, **sedimentary** and **metamorphic** rocks. Igneous rocks are made from **magma**, a hot liquid rock found deep in the Earth's crust. Sedimentary rocks are made from **particles**, such as sand and broken shells. Metamorphic rocks are made when other rocks change their form (see pages 20-21).

▶ These rocks, called the Mittens, are found in Monument Valley in Arizona, USA. They are made from sedimentary rocks, including sandstone and shale.

Oldest and youngest rocks

The oldest rocks in the world are found in north-west Canada. They are metamorphic rocks formed more than 4 billion years ago. The oldest sedimentary rocks are about 3.5 billion years old and they are found in Australia and Southern Africa. The youngest rocks are those which have only just formed, for example igneous rocks formed from the **lava** produced by volcanoes, such as those on the island of Sicily, from the **eruptions** of Mount Etna.

Q What is the most common mineral on Earth?
A Quartz. This is a mineral that is made of silicon dioxide. Sand is made from quartz and sand is used in the making of glass, concrete and china. Large **crystals** of quartz are used as gemstones.

▲ Rose-coloured quartz is used in jewellery.

▲ Granite is an igneous rock.

▲ Limestone is a sedimentary rock.

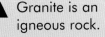

◀ Marble is a metamorphic rock.

Inside the Earth

Amazingly, the ground beneath our feet is moving. You cannot feel it, but it is moving all the time. The surface of the Earth is formed from a layer called the crust. Beneath the crust are two other layers, the **mantle** and the **core**.

Red-hot core

The core is at the centre of the Earth. Here, temperatures reach 3,700°C. The inner core is a solid ball of metal, mostly iron and **nickel**. The outer core is made of liquid rock.

The mantle

The Earth's middle layer, the mantle, is about 2,900 km thick and is made up of rock. In some places, the rock is so hot that it melts and becomes liquid, like a thick soup. This is called magma. **Currents** of magma rise up through the mantle to the crust, where they cool and then sink again.

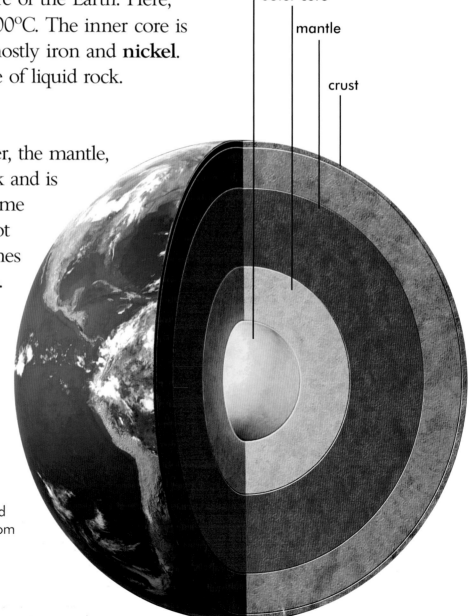

inner core

outer core

mantle

crust

▶ Inside the Earth are three layers: the crust, mantle and core. The core is formed from two layers, the inner and outer core.

The Earth's crust

The outer layer or crust is made up of large **plates** that float on the mantle. The plates that make up the land are up to 30 km thick, while the **oceanic plates** are thinner, less than 12 km thick. Currents inside the mantle cause the plates to move. As a result, some plates are **colliding,** while others are pulling away from each other.

Q What is the 'Ring of Fire'?

A This is the circle of volcanoes that occur around the Pacific Ocean. Movements of the Pacific plate against neighbouring plates produce earthquakes and volcanoes in this region.

▼ Mountains form when two plates push against each other, causing the rocks to crumple.

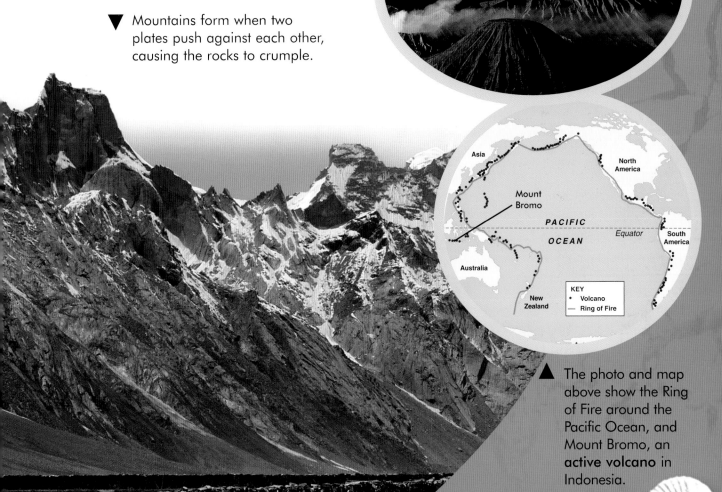

Asia

North America

Mount Bromo

PACIFIC

OCEAN

Equator

South America

Australia

New Zealand

KEY
• Volcano
— Ring of Fire

▲ The photo and map above show the Ring of Fire around the Pacific Ocean, and Mount Bromo, an **active volcano** in Indonesia.

Rock cycles

The rock cycle is a series of changes in which rocks are formed, broken down and changed into other rocks. The starting point is magma that forms in the mantle. Cracks in the crust allow some of the magma to escape to the surface where it becomes lava and then igneous rock.

Rock is broken up by wind and water, and small particles are washed away

3

Lava quickly cools and turns into black igneous rock

Most of the magma cools underground to become igneous rock

The igneous cycle

Movements in the crust push the igneous rocks down into the mantle where they melt and become magma again

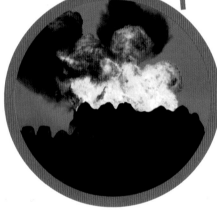

2

A volcano forms where lava erupts from the ground

Sometimes, heat and **pressure** in the ground cause igneous and sedimentary rock to change into metamorphic rock

1

Cycles within cycles

There are mini cycles within the rock cycle called the igneous and sedimentary rock cycles. Also, igneous and sedimentary rocks can both be changed into metamorphic rocks.

7

4

Rock particles are carried by rivers into the oceans where they sink to the sea bed. Layers of **sediment** build up and become sedimentary rock

5

Eventually, the rock particles become new sedimentary rocks

The sedimentary cycle

Sedimentary rocks at the surface are broken up by the action of wind, rain and Sun

6

Volcanoes

A volcanic eruption occurs when lava, together with **ash** and gas, erupts at the Earth's surface. Sometimes the volcanic eruption is violent and lava is thrown high into the air. Other eruptions are less violent and lava just oozes out of cracks in the ground. The lava then cools and turns into a solid rock called **basalt**.

Volcano shapes

Volcanoes are made from layers of lava that have built up over many eruptions. The shape of a volcano depends on the type of lava. Runny lava forms a low, gently sloping shape that is called a **shield volcano**, for example the volcanoes found on the island of Hawaii. Thick, sticky lava does not flow easily, so it forms a **cone-shaped volcano**, such as Mount Fuji in Japan.

▼ Magma is a thick liquid that contains gases and fragments of rock. It collects inside the volcano before it erupts.

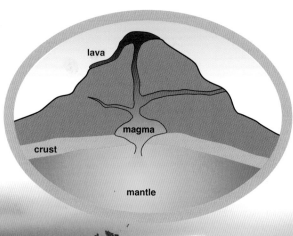

Active or extinct

Active volcanoes are those that have erupted during the last few thousand years, for example Mount Etna in Sicily and Mount Teide in Tenerife. An **extinct volcano** is one that has not erupted during the last few thousand to 10,000 years.

▼ Mount Teide, on Tenerife, one of the Canary Islands, is 3,718 metres high.

Q. What is a caldera?

A. This is a huge **crater** that forms when the top of the volcano collapses either during or after an eruption. Sometimes it fills with water to form a crater lake.

▲ A caldera in Japan.

▲ In the lava flow above, the lava is red-hot at the edges. As it cools, it hardens and turns into black igneous rock.

Underwater volcanoes

There are more than 5,000 volcanoes under the seas and oceans, such as Kolumbo near the Greek island of Santorini in the Mediterranean. The cone of this volcano suddenly appeared above the water in 1649, and the eruption killed 70 islanders.

Making igneous rocks

Only a small fraction of the Earth's magma rises to the surface and escapes as lava. Most remains underground, where it cools to form igneous rocks.

Cooling underground

Magma moves towards the surface through cracks in the crust. Eventually, the cracks stop and the magma is trapped. The hot magma cools very slowly and becomes solid rock.

▼ These mountains in Chile are formed from granite, a type of igneous rock.

Q and A

Crystals

Crystals form as the magma cools. The size of the crystals depends on how quickly it cools. Large crystals form when the magma cools very slowly, for example the crystals in gabbro and granite. Fast cooling produces small crystals, for example in basalt.

Hot rocks

In some parts of the world, hot igneous rocks lie close to the Earth's surface. The rocks heat water in the ground and wells can be dug to reach the hot pools. In other places, hot water bubbles out of the ground forming geysers and hot water pools, which can be used to produce electricity.

▼ Steam rising from hot pools in Yellowstone Park, USA.

Q What is a geyser?

A A geyser is a jet of hot water and steam that spurts from the ground. The water is heated by hot rocks below the surface. One of the world's best-known geysers is Old Faithful in Yellowstone National Park in the USA. It erupts every 60 to 90 minutes, sending thousands of litres of hot water high into the air.

▲ Old Faithful geyser erupting.

Rocks under water

Rivers carry a lot of sediment, such as sand, **silt** and clay, that has been washed into the water. These particles are the raw materials to make new sedimentary rocks.

Mud on the sea bed

The sediment carried by rivers ends up in the sea, where it drops to the sea bed. Beneath the surface of the sea bed are many layers of sediment that have built up over millions of years. As more sediment lands on the sea bed, the lower layers get squashed. The weight pushing down on the sediment causes the water to be squeezed out. When this happens, salts in the sediment form crystals. The salt crystals help to glue the particles together and form sedimentary rock.

▼ Mudflats on a river estuary at low tide. Some of the mud will be washed into the ocean where it will sink to the sea bed.

▼ These rocks in Australia, called the Twelve Apostles, are formed from limestone, a type of sedimentary rock. The rocks have been broken up by the waves, forming **stacks**.

stacks

Q and A

Clues in rocks

Sedimentary rocks form over hundreds of millions of years, and during this time the sediments change. This is due to changes in **climate** and vegetation. This means a sequence of different sedimentary rocks is formed. **Geologists** can study the sequence of rocks in a cliff to find out about the climate millions of years ago.

Q How do rocks tells us what happened to the dinosaurs?

A Scientists believe that a huge **meteor** hit the Earth, wiping out many plant and animal species, including the dinosaurs. By testing sedimentary rocks for iridium, a substance found in meteors, scientists have proved that a huge meteor hit the Earth about 65 million years ago.

▼ The cliffs of the Grand Canyon in the USA are made up of layers of sedimentary rock that were formed under the sea. The rocks at the top are about 270 million years old. Those at the bottom were formed more than 600 million years ago.

limestone
270 million years

sandstone
275 million years

shale,
280 million years

limestone
340 million years

shale
550 million years

Sedimentary rocks

There are many different types of sedimentary rock. They differ in the type of particles from which they are made.

Limestone

Limestone rocks are rich in a mineral called **calcite**, which contains calcium carbonate. This is because they are made up mostly of the crushed shells of sea animals, such as molluscs, that died millions of years ago. Chalk is a type of limestone. It is made from the skeletons of tiny animals too small to be seen with the human eye.

▼ These cliffs are made of chalk, a soft white rock. Chalk crumbles easily so it can be use to write on blackboards.

Q and A

Q What is a **fossil**?

A A fossil is the preserved remains of an animal or plant in a rock. A fossil forms when the remains of an animal drop to the bottom of a lake or ocean and the soft parts of the body are broken down. The hard parts, such as bones or shell, become covered in mud and sand and eventually become part of the rock.

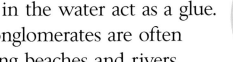

Sandstone

Sandstone is made from grains of sand. A grain of sand is made from quartz (see page 5), a common mineral. The grains are stuck together by **silica**.

Conglomerate

Conglomerate is a knobbly rock made up of stones, pebbles and gravel that have become glued together. Minerals such as silica or calcium carbonate in the water act as a glue. Conglomerates are often found along beaches and rivers.

▲ Fossil fish.

Shale

Shale is a soft rock made from fine grains of clay. It is the most common sedimentary rock and is found around the world. It is used in brick-making and construction.

Folding and faulting

The plates that make up the Earth's crust are moving all the time. When this happens, the rocks along the edges of the crust become stretched and squeezed.

Folds

When the plates move, some of the rocks are pushed up and the layers, instead of lying horizontally, are pushed upwards or even become **folded**.

rock layers

rocks pushed up from below

▼ These rocks made from mudstone and shale have been pushed so that the layers are almost vertical.

▲ Folds form when the rocks are pushed upwards by movements in the Earth's crust.

Faults

The forces that move the plates are so powerful that huge masses of rock can split and move apart. Imagine you are trying to break a pencil. First, you apply a lot of force with both hands and the pencil bends. Then, the pencil snaps in the middle. This happens in rocks. Great pressure is applied, and suddenly the rocks break and slide past each other. This is called **shearing** and it creates a **fault** or a break in the rock.

Q What causes earthquakes?

A An earthquake occurs when two plates suddenly slide past each other, causing a release of energy and a **shock wave** that shakes the ground. Most earthquakes are too small to be noticed, but a major earthquake can cause huge damage and loss of life.

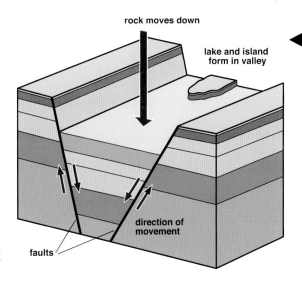

rock moves down

lake and island form in valley

direction of movement

faults

◀ The Rift Valley in Africa was formed when two faults appeared in the rock and the block of rock in the middle dropped to create a deep valley.

▲ This building has been badly damaged by an earthquake.

Mountain building

When two plates push against each other, the rocks crumple and are pushed upwards to form mountains. For example, the Himalayan Mountains were formed over millions of years when the Indian plate collided with the Asiatic plate. These movements are still taking place, as the Himalayas are becoming taller by a few centimetres each year.

Re-made rocks

The extreme heat and pressure that exist far beneath the Earth's surface can change the structure and appearance of rocks. This creates metamorphic rocks such as **gneiss** and marble.

Crushed and squeezed

Rocks can also be changed by crushing and squeezing, processes that take place deep in the ground over several million years. Even the shape of the particles can be altered, from round to almost flat. Both igneous and sedimentary rocks can change form when placed under pressure. When sandstone is changed to quartzite, the layers disappear and the crystals melt and re-form.

▲ Granite can be changed into gneiss. Gneiss consists of alternating bands of dark and light minerals.

▼ An ancient gneiss stone circle at Callanish on the Isle of Lewis in Scotland which was built over 4,000 years ago.

Q and A

Marble

High temperatures and pressure can change limestone into marble. Marble is a popular building material because it can be rubbed to give a shiny, hard surface. It is a harder rock than limestone, but not as hard as granite. There are many different types of marble, each named after the place where it is found. The best-quality marble comes from Carrara in Italy and it has been used in many buildings and sculptures in Europe.

Q What is slate?

A Slate is a layered metamorphic rock that is made from shale. The layers split apart easily, and form thin sheets that can be used for roof tiles.

▼ A marble **quarry** in Carrara, Italy.

▼ The Leaning Tower of Pisa is built of white Carrara marble.

▲ Slate roof tiles.

21

Weathered rocks

Rocks do not remain the same for ever. When they are exposed to the weather – the Sun, rain and wind – they start to change. This is called **weathering**.

Sun and wind

Rocks in the desert become very hot during the day and they **expand**. At night, temperatures fall and the rocks shrink. This constant expansion and **contraction** causes thin layers of rock to peel away from the surface. This is a form of **physical weathering**. Wind can also wear away the surface of a rock.

▼ The spectacular Wave Rock in Arizona, USA, is formed from sandstone that has been physically weathered by the wind that swirls around the rocks.

Q and A

Freeze and thaw

Freeze-thaw weathering occurs in places where water freezes. Water trickles through cracks in the rocks, and on cold nights it freezes. Water expands as it freezes and the force of the expanding ice causes the cracks to become larger. Then the ice thaws (melts) and the water can go even further into the rock. Eventually, the rock breaks apart.

Rain and weathering

Rain simply falling on to the surface of some rocks can gradually wear away the surface. This is because rainwater is not pure water. It contains substances such as weak acids. When rainwater falls on limestone and chalk rocks, the acid reacts with the calcium carbonate and slowly wears away the surface. This is called **chemical weathering**.

Q How does a rock arch form?

A A rock **arch** is formed by the process of weathering. The wind blows sand over the surface of rocks, and this wears away the softer rocks, leaving the harder rocks. One of the best-known rock arches is Delicate Arch in Utah, USA. It is made from sandstone and is one of more than 2,000 natural arches in Arches National Park.

▲ Delicate Arch in Utah, USA.

◀ This narrow passageway, called Antelope Canyon in Arizona, USA, has been formed by torrents of water wearing away the rock.

Erosion

Once a rock has been weathered into small pieces, the pieces may be moved to another place by the wind or water. This is called **erosion**.

Erosion often takes place at the same time as weathering. Weathering produces the small pieces of rock that are carried away or eroded by wind and water, and this exposes fresh rock to be weathered.

Retreating cliffs

Cliffs along the coasts are constantly battered by the sea, especially during storms. The force of the waves smashes rocks against cliffs, wearing away the rock at the bottom. Eventually, so much rock has been removed from the bottom that the rest of the cliff collapses. Cliffs made of soft rocks, such as clay, retreat more quickly than those made of harder rocks.

▼ These cliffs are formed from soft chalk rock, which is being worn away by the waves.

Sandy beaches

The swirling sea water grinds smaller pieces of rocks together, so they become smaller and rounder, creating pebbles and eventually sand. When the waves retreat back down the beach, they carry the pebbles and sand away. The sand and pebbles are dropped further along the coast where they form beaches. Depending on the **tides**, some beaches gain sand from elsewhere, while others continually lose their sand.

Q What is a groyne?

A A groyne is a narrow barrier which extends down the beach into the sea to stop the tide carrying away sand and pebbles. It is built from materials such as rock, wood or concrete. Groynes are part of the coastal defences built along coastlines that are being eroded.

tide carries sand in this direction

sand is dropped here

▲ The groynes on this beach prevent the sand from being carried away with the tide.

▲ Sand is carried along this coast by the tides. The bar of sand is getting longer as more sand is added to the end.

Soil

Soil covers much of the surface of the land. It is formed of particles of weathered rock mixed with **organic material**, which is material that was once living, such as dead leaves.

Sand, silt and clay

Soil contains a mix of sand, silt and clay. Sand is the largest of the three particles. These particles come from the weathering of rocks. A clay soil does not allow water to drain easily through it. In contrast, a sandy soil allows water to drain easily, but the soil dries up in summer. **Loam** has a good mix of sand, silt and clay and this creates a soil that is good for growing crops.

▲ Plant roots grow through soil and take up water and **nutrients** from it.

▼ Farmers use a plough to turn over the soil so that it is ready to sow seeds.

Humus

Fallen leaves and other parts of plants break down to form **humus**. Humus is good for the soil. It helps to increase the drainage, makes the soil easier to work and provides nutrients to the plants.

Soil erosion

Soil needs protection from the weather. This is usually provided by plant cover as their roots hold the soil together. However, if the plant cover is removed, the soil is exposed to the weather. Then the soil may be washed or blown away. This is called soil erosion.

Q What is a soil profile?

A This is a vertical cut made down through the soil to the rock, which reveals all the different layers that make up the soil. A good, loamy soil used for farming will extend deep into the ground, but some soils are really thin, such as those that occur over chalk.

▶ Water has washed away the soil beneath these trees, leaving the roots exposed.

▲ The spade shows the depth of this soil.

Rocks and people

Rocks are an important part of the landscape, creating mountains and cliffs and many other features. They have many uses. They are dug from the ground and used in buildings, roads, roofs and even jewellery. However, rocks can be damaged by the activities of people.

Rock mining

Rocks are usually quarried from the ground, using dynamite to break up the rock. Some of the rock is crushed to use in concrete or roads, while blocks may be cut for use in buildings or as roof tiles.

▼ Mountains and rocky landscapes are popular tourist attractions. However, too many tourists can lead to damage to the surfaces of rocks.

Q and A

Acid rain

Acid rain is a form of air pollution and it can damage rock (see page 23). Rain is slightly **acidic**, but pollution from cars and industry increases the amount of acidity in rain. When acid rain falls on buildings made from soft rocks such as limestone, it causes more weathering. This damage is worldwide and can be seen on cathedrals and castles in Western Europe, in the Parthenon in Athens, Greece and the Pyramids in Egypt.

Q Is air pollution damaging the Taj Mahal?

A Yes. The Taj Mahal in India is built from strong white marble but air pollution from heavy traffic and nearby industry is causing damage. Cracks are appearing in the walls and the white marble has dirty stains. The Indian government is working to improve air quality and to save the building from further damage.

◄ The Parthenon in Athens has been badly damaged by air pollution created by the heavy traffic in the city.

▲ Damaged stone at the Taj Mahal being repaired.

▲ The Taj Mahal in India was built in the 1640s. It is considered to be one of the world's most beautiful buildings.

Glossary

acidic containing acid

acid rain rain that is more acidic than normal due to the presence of weak acids; a type of air pollution produced by burning coal and oil, which damages rocks

active volcano a volcano that has erupted in the last 10,000 years

arch a curved shape, like an up-side-down U

ash particles of rock thrown out during a volcanic eruption

basalt an igneous rock, usually formed when lava cools and becomes solid

biotite a dark mineral found in igneous and metamorphic rocks

calcite a type of mineral made of calcium carbonate, found in limestone, chalk and marble

calcium carbonate the substance that forms chalk and limestone

chemical weathering the breakdown of rocks caused by the substances found in rainwater such as acids

climate the regular pattern of weather experienced in a particular place over a long period of time

collide to crash together

cone-shaped volcano a volcano with tapering sides that form a point

contraction to become shallower or smaller

core the centre of the Earth

crater a bowl-shaped hole or opening at the top of a volcano

crust the outer layer of the Earth

crystal a solid formed when a liquid cools, often having a shiny appearance

current the flow of liquid in a particular direction

erosion the wearing away of rock by wind and water

eruption the release of lava and ash from a volcano

expand to increase in size or volume

extinct volcano a volcano that has not erupted during the last 10,000 years

fault a large crack or break through a mass of rock

feldspar a common mineral containing silicon, found in igneous rocks. When it is weathered it forms clays

folded a bend in a layer of rocks

fossil the preserved remains of prehistoric animals and plants

geologist a person who studies rocks

gneiss a metamorphic rock, formed from granite, with bands of light and dark minerals

granite a type of igneous rock with large crystals of quartz, which is widely used for building

humus organic matter, such as decayed leaves, that forms part of the soil

igneous rock a type of rock formed from magma when it cools and becomes solid

lava the liquid rock, called magma, that erupts from volcanoes

limestone a type of sedimentary rock

loam a type of soil

magma liquid rock beneath the Earth's surface

mantle the thick layer of hot rock beneath the Earth's crust

meteors lumps of rocks that enter the Earth's atmosphere from space

metamorphic rock rocks that have undergone change

mineral a natural substance in the ground

nickel a metal with a silvery appearance

nutrient a substance needed by plants and animals for healthy growth; plants get their nutrients from the soil

oceanic plates parts of the Earth's crust under the oceans

organic material matter that was once living, for example dead leaves

particle a tiny piece of rock

physical weathering the breakdown of rocks by Sun, wind and water

plate part of the Earth's crust

pressure a pushing force on a surface, such as the weight of rocks near the surface pushing down on rocks below

quarry a place where rocks are dug from the ground

quartz a type of mineral

sediment particles of sand, silt and clay that are carried by water and which settle on the bed of a river, lake or ocean

sedimentary rock rock made from layers of sediment

shearing when two huge blocks of rock slide past each other

shield volcano a volcano with a shallow or low shape

shock wave a vibration that travels through the ground after an earthquake or volcanic eruption

silica a glass-like substance found in magma, the common name of silicon dioxide

silt small particles of sand

stack a steep column of rock in the sea found near a coast. It is created when the rocks of a cliff are eroded, leaving just the stack

tides the daily rise and fall of the sea along the coast

weathering the breaking down of rocks when they are exposed to the weather

Further reading

The Rock Cycle, Sally Morgan (Wayland, 2008)
Rocks and Minerals, Chris Pellant (Dorling Kindersley, 2000)
Crystals (Geology Rocks!), Rebecca Faulkner (Raintree, 2008)

Websites

Good informative site with useful animations on the rock cycle.
Mineralogy 4 Kids: www.minsocam.org/MSA/K12/K_12.html

Informative website on rocks and minerals.
Rocks for Kids: www.rocksforkids.com

Fun website in which junior rock hunters provide lots of facts about rocks, volcanoes, inside the Earth and much more.
Welcome to our Earth: www.fi.edu/fellows/fellow4/nov98/index.html

Index